All About Science

Magnetism

Angela Royston

raintree

a Capstone company — publishers for children

Raintree is an imprint of Capstone Global Library Limited, a company incorporated in England and Wales having its registered office at 265 Banbury Road, Oxford OX2 7DY – Registered company number: 6695582

www.raintree.co.uk
myorders@raintree.co.uk

Text © Capstone Global Library Limited 2016
First published in hardback in 2016
The moral rights of the proprietor have been asserted.

Edited by Linda Staniford
Designed by Steve Mead
Picture research by Kelly Garvin
Production by Victoria Fitzgerald
Originated by Capstone Global Library Ltd
Printed and bound in China

ISBN 978 1 474 71421 1
19 18 17 16 15
10 9 8 7 6 5 4 3 2 1

British Library Cataloguing in Publication Data
A full catalogue record for this book is available from the British Library.

Acknowledgements
We would like to thank the following for permission to reproduce photographs:
Capstone Press/Karon Dubke, 4, 6, 7, 8, 12, 13, 14, 15, 16, 17, 18, 19, 20, 21, 26, 29; Corbis/Lance Iverson/San Francisco Chronicle, 11; Glow Images/Gavin Hellier/Robert Harding, 23; iStockphoto: colematt, 5; Science Source/Lawrence Lawry, cover; Shutterstock: AlexLMX, 24, dvande, 10, mamahoohooba, 22, Opka, 25, rayjunk, 27

We would like to thank Pat O'Mahony for his help in the preparation of this book.

Every effort has been made to contact copyright holders of material reproduced in this book. Any omissions will be rectified in subsequent printings if notice is given to the publisher.

All the Internet addresses (URLs) given in this book were valid at the time of going to press. However, due to the dynamic nature of the Internet, some addresses may have changed, or sites may have changed or ceased to exist since publication. While the author and publisher regret any inconvenience this may cause readers, no responsibility for any such changes can be accepted by either the author or the publisher.

Contents

What is magnetism? 4

Shapes of magnets..6

Using magnets 10

Exploring magnetic force 12

What can magnetic force pass through? 16

North and south poles.................................... 20

Maglev train 22

Earth is a magnet.. 24

Using a compass.. 26

Experiment results... 28

Quiz... 29

Glossary 30

Find out more... 31

Index... 32

Some words are shown in bold, **like this**. You can find out what they mean by looking in the glossary.

What is magnetism?

A magnet has a force that pulls certain objects towards it. For example, fridge and freezer doors have a rubbery strip around the edge. The strip contains a magnet, which pulls the door tight shut.

magnetic strip

A magnet strip around the edge of the fridge door keeps the door shut.

Magnetism works even when the magnet is not touching the object. If the magnet is close enough, it pulls the object towards it.

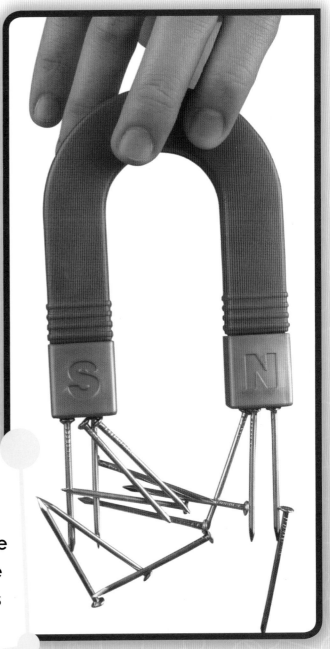

The magnet's magnetic force begins to lift the nails before the magnet touches them.

5

Shapes of magnets

Most magnets are shaped like a bar or a horseshoe. The magnetic force is strongest at the ends of these magnets. Ring magnets are round with a hole in the middle, like a doughnut.

Big magnets are stronger than small magnets.

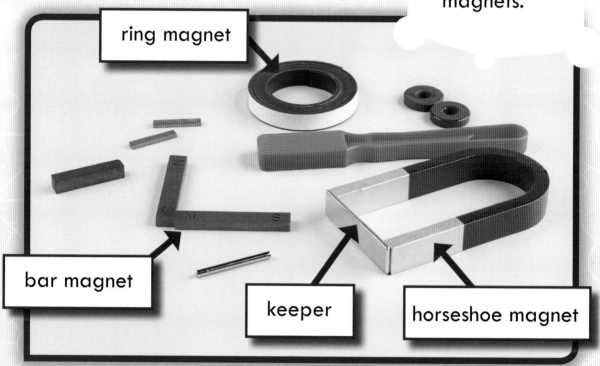

ring magnet

bar magnet

keeper

horseshoe magnet

This little plastic man has small magnets hidden inside his hands.

When a bar or horseshoe magnet is not being used, a metal bar is placed across the ends. The bar is called a **keeper** and it stops the magnetic force leaking away.

Magnetic or non-magnetic?

Materials that are attracted to a magnet are called magnetic. Materials that are not attracted to a magnet are non-magnetic. Test some objects for magnetism with this magnet test.

You will need:

✓ a magnet

✓ objects made of different materials, such as plastic blocks, wooden toy, paper card, nail, empty drinks can

1 Make a table like the one shown here.

2 Test each material with the magnet and fill in the table.

Material	Magnetic	Non-magnetic
plastic blocks		
wooden toy		
paper card		
nail		
empty drinks can		

Check your results on page 28.

Using magnets

Magnets are used in many different ways. Some toy trains use magnets to connect the wagons. Pouches for smart phones may use magnets to close them easily.

A very strong magnet lifts a heavy load of crushed scrap metal.

A magnet sorts non-magnetic aluminium cans from steel cans.

Iron and steel are magnetic. All other materials and most other metals are non-magnetic. This allows **recycling centres** to use magnets to separate iron and steel from other **scrap metal**.

Exploring magnetic force

When something magnetic is attached to a magnet, it becomes a temporary magnet. For example, a metal paperclip attached to a magnet becomes a temporary magnet. It can then **attract** another metal paperclip.

You need a strong magnet to make a long chain of steel paperclips.

To make a nail into a magnet, keep stroking it in the same direction with a magnet.

When the paperclip is separated from the main magnet, it stops being a temporary magnet. You can also make something magnetic, such as a paperclip or nail, into a magnet by stroking it with a permanent magnet.

Which magnet is the strongest?

You will need:

✓ 3 or 4 magnets of different size and shape

✓ a nail

✓ a sheet of paper

✓ a ruler and pencil

1 Draw a line across the paper and place the nail on it as shown in the photo.

2 Slowly move the first magnet across the paper towards the line.

3 Mark the place where the magnet begins to move the nail.

4 Repeat with the other magnets. Which magnet is the strongest?

Check your results on page 28.

What can magnetic force pass through?

A magnet can **attract** a magnetic object even when there is a gap between them. This means that magnetic force can pass through air. It can also pass through other materials, including paper, water and glass.

Small magnets can hold a sheet of paper on to a metal door.

As the magnet is lowered into the water, its magnetic force lifts the screw.

A weak magnetic force can only pass through a thin layer of material. Strong magnetic forces can work across bigger gaps and through thicker materials.

The poles of a magnet

Magnetic force is strongest at the ends of a magnet. The ends are called the **poles.** Explore what happens when you put the poles of two magnets together.

You will need:
✓ two bar magnets

1 Bring one end of one magnet towards one end of the other. What happens?

Most tacks stick to the ends or poles of the magnet.

2 Turn one of the magnets around and move the other end towards the first magnet. What happens now?

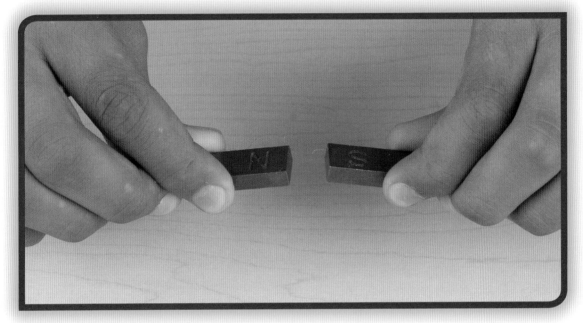

Do the ends pull together or push each other apart?

3 What happens when you turn both magnets around?

Check your results on page 28.

North and south poles

Every magnet has a north **pole** and a south pole. When the north pole of one magnet is moved towards the south pole of another magnet, the magnets are pulled, or **attracted**, towards each other.

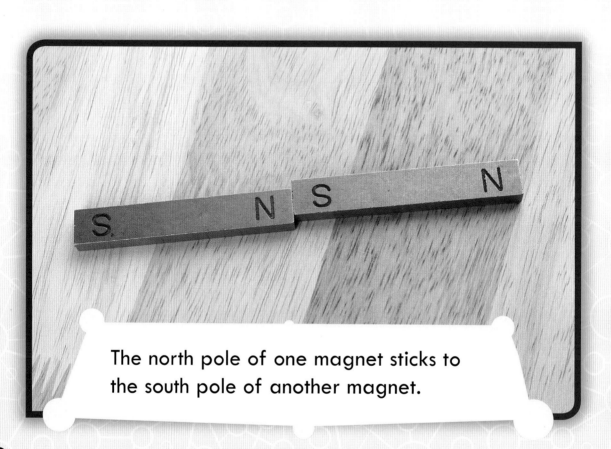

The north pole of one magnet sticks to the south pole of another magnet.

Can you make two like poles touch each other?

When you move two north poles or two south poles together, they push each other away. Like poles **repel** each other, but unlike poles attract.

Maglev train

Maglev trains are extremely fast and have no wheels. They move so fast because they do not touch the track. Instead they lift up a short way and "fly" through the air.

A Maglev train is driven by the force of magnetism.

A Maglev train floats just above the track.

A Maglev train has large magnets underneath it. The track includes electric coils, which become magnets when electricity flows through them. The coils **repel** the magnets under the train to lift it up.

Earth is a magnet

The Earth is a giant magnet. The rocks around the centre of the Earth are made mostly of hot, liquid iron. The iron forms a huge magnet.

The rocks in the middle of the Earth contain lots of iron, which has become magnetized.

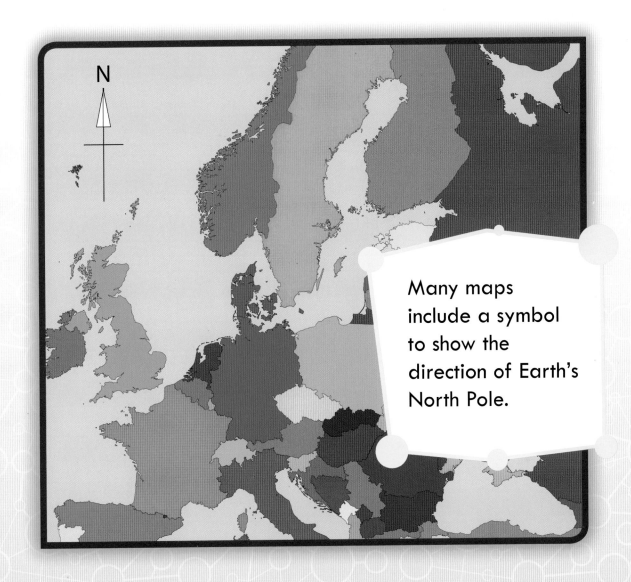

Many maps include a symbol to show the direction of Earth's North Pole.

The Earth's magnet has two **poles**, one at each end. One points to the North Pole in the Arctic. The other pole points to the South Pole in Antarctica.

Using a compass

A **compass** helps people to find their way. It has a magnet in the shape of a needle, which rotates around its centre. When the needle comes to rest, it lines up with the Earth's magnet and so points to north.

The compass is turned until north on the compass lies at the end of the needle.

A hiker turns the map until the symbol for north points the same way as the compass needle.

Many people use information beamed from **satellites** to find their way. But aircraft pilots, ship crews and many hikers still use a compass to keep them on course.

Experiment results
What happened?

Magnetic or non-magnetic (page 8)

Only objects made of certain metals, usually iron and steel, are magnetic. Most materials are not magnetic.

Which magnet is the strongest? (page 14)

The strongest magnet is the one whose magnetic force moves the nail from farthest away.

The poles of a magnet (page 18)

Whichever way you turn the magnets around, opposite **poles** will **attract** each other and like poles will **repel** each other (see page 20).

Quiz

1 Aluminium and plastic are
   a both magnetic
   b both non-magnetic
   c one is magnetic but not the other

2 The magnet can attract the screw through water.
   a true
   b false

3 A **Maglev train** is driven by
   a magnetic force
   b electricity
   c diesel oil

Turn to page 31 for the answers.

Glossary

attract pull towards something

compass device that shows the direction of the North Pole

keeper iron bar placed against the ends of a magnet when it is not being used to help keep its magnetism

Maglev train train that is driven by magnetic force

pole end of a magnet where the magnetic force is strongest

recycling centre place where materials are processed so that they can be used again

repel push something away

satellite object in space which travels around a much larger object, such as the Earth

scrap metal things made of metal which have been thrown away

Find out more

Books

Fizzing Physics (Science Crackers), Steve Parker (QED, 2012)

Forces and Magnets (Moving up with Science), Peter Riley (Franklin Watts, 2015)

Utterly Amazing Science, Robert Winston (Dorling Kindersley 2014)

Websites

www.bbc.co.uk/bitesize/ks2/science/physical_processes/magnets/play/
You might have to try all the options in this tricky game!

www.first4magnets.com/fun-magnet-facts-for-kids-i77
This website has some short, sharp facts about magnets.

www.sciencekids.co.nz/gamesactivities/magnetssprings.html
This website has a game exploring magnetic force.

Answers: 1b, 2a, 3a

Index

aluminium 11

attract 12, 16, 20, 21

bar magnet 6, 7, 18, 19

compass 26, 27

Earth 24, 25, 26

horseshoe magnet 6, 7

iron 11, 24

keeper 6, 7

Maglev train 22, 23

magnetic force 4, 5, 6, 7, 12, 16, 17, 18, 22

magnetic materials 8, 9, 11

making a magnet 12, 13

non-magnetic materials 8, 11

poles 18, 20, 21, 25

recycling centres 11

repel 21, 23

ring magnet 6

satellites 27

scrap metal 10, 11

steel 11, 12

temporary magnet 12, 13

uses of magnets 10, 11